BELL LAP

LAURA WINBERRY

INDOLENT BOOKS

Cover photo: Kent Baumgardt
Cover design: adam b. bohannon
Book design: Nieves Guerra
Book editor: Lisa DeSiro

Published by Indolent Books,
an imprint of Indolent Arts Foundation, Inc.

www.indolentbooks.com
Brooklyn, New York
ISBN: 978-1-945023-12-5

to my wolfpack, my dears
(my sugarskulld / slick diamond-boned / thick mistresses):
toes on the line

CONTENTS

Let me tell you what I think of bicycling. I think it has done more to emancipate women than anything else in the world. It gives women a feeling of freedom and self-reliance. I stand and rejoice every time I see a woman ride by on a wheel… the picture of free, untrammeled womanhood.
–Susan B. Anthony

bell lap (n.): *The final lap in a race of repeated circuits, signaled by the ringing of a bell.*

the warm up

(meet me on the edge)

of 5th / I'm a mess
dressed in fresh lime peels, precious
metal & $$$$$

early fall through mid-winter
the days become expend expand
everything: gather-gather

finding the human edge in our blood-story

every weekend the location shifts
and we follow the carnival of cyclocross
a clump of minnows shoaling in the rain

coffee like ichor in our veins
we eat weird gel things
watermelon   chocolate   espresso-flavored orgasm

suck down
gummy block-sugar

before the gunshot splits the hush

                    viewed from above
                    cyclocross is a sprawling Richard Scarry scene
little animals
                    sloppy-parading a pop-up town

                    telescoping in the set comes into focus:
                    it's an eighth grader's diorama
                    on Ancient Greece (shaken
dropped
                    left out in the rain)

                    all of us a tangle
                    of figurines spilling out wet
                    exposed knuckles seeping thinly
gloved
                    our eyes wide-searching
                    from behind taut cellophane lenses

                    printed numbers safety-pinned over shoulders   flanks
                    our backs bent over

                    handlebars
                    body-velum spandex we
                    creatures of the alley

                    fembot hustlers in
                    disguise—at a carnival
                    of skinned vixenleg

Athena was no figurine
at her birth she gushed forth fully armed
from the head of her father Zeus

(wow)

what if we all made our debuts with such poise and capacity

sure
Athena had her opposition cut out for her

but where were we born
what were we born into

how many of us
stitched into thighs   skulls
were brandishing thunderbolts
before we'd even sucked
our first bubbles of raw air

my Eves
my difficult-sweet Eves dressed in tattered evening
gowns   mud-encrusted tiaras made of polymer

                                        a strap around the chin

        fresh skin

cleated feet like hooves
clicking into place at the sound of a gunshot cleaving rain   and hush

my chest-deep creatures with crystal

                                rib cages that hold
                                that won't back down despite his-
                                story / tamp / quiet

my tender herd of sweat
I cannot forget our tangle:
of hair   teeth   muscle and ache
of all that swims beneath our meat

how stunning
to be sphinxes one day

                                a crumple of splinter and beams the next

and still capable of coming out swinging
in the bell lap legs fracking   pedals   spokes
our eyes zeroed in   on the pixelated future

where the earth still spins   and we diverge still reeling
from how did it all happen   so goddamned fast

my lacuna of blood-Eves
are you still here
I think I am

once a pack always a crushed honeycomb

a family   a sharp lamb

though the venue changes every weekend, the spirit of cyclocross motors on unruffled: gather the animals, pray for storm, turn the body inside out. also: don't stop pedaling. ever. unless it's to wrap a fist around a few dollar bills protruding like mangy seedlings from mud or cleavage or someone's G-string.

Belgium is the Fertile Crescent of the 'cross world and the Euro-Belgies breed and are bred for the sport. but it's American fans who first added $ bill hand-ups to the mix. which quickly eroded into thong-ups and teeth-ups and dirty money everywhere. from grassroots gatherings to national championships, a 'cross race is no longer a 'cross race without several Washingtons folded lengthwise, waiting to be snatched.

what's our axis
our access

as women where do we figure ourselves
onto the stage and its pageant
of dancing bears

only they aren't dancing bears
they're animals with questions

and ache

damp pelts
scratching to get out

they're you

                                            me

                        the whole world

years spread their legs

between today and the lone 19th-century French soldier
who first pedaled slick
cow pasture for sport his routes were thick
were wet grass were
earthen obstacles ditches ravines
canals were snow-hail and rain-sleet

centuries later
iterations of his shoddy routes
swallow hours of our lives

we give up lovers
boyfriends jobs to burst
our pink pretty-slate lungs
through zipped-up jerseys
and skinsuits

           damp with the bouquet
           of: seared boar, ale & frite-smoke /
           sweaty persistence

replete with counter-culture, costumery, and antics, and despite being droll, 'cross is cutthroat as fuck. it'll put a fist in your face and pip you at the line or: maybe that's just all bike racing. still, humans are adept at being humans and making a competition out of anything, especially themselves. when this happens in 'cross, pre-race preparation can and does get serious:

23 psi or 21. file tread or mud tread or one of each. two caffeinated gels and two puffs from the inhaler or inhaler plus a triple shot of single-origin espresso. rollers or trainer or course pre-ride. full strength embrocation or mellow. wool base layer or mesh. brown-tinted sunglasses or rose-tinted sunglasses or clear. long sleeve skinsuit or three-quarter length, insulated long sleeve skinsuit or short sleeves with arm warmers. knee warmers or more embro plus an epidermis of vaseline. more food or less food or more. was that enough sleep or too much. put the legs up or pre-ride the course for the fifth time. more water, more Gatorade, more coffee. more Porta-Potty. or just go in the grass over there because the line's too long because everyone else is also over-hydrated and has the pre-race shits. longer warm-up or shorter warm-up or no warm-up at all or go to the bathroom again. no, yes. wait, yup, yes: go to the bathroom. is it time yet, is it time yet, is it time yet, I don't feel good, I think I'm going to shit my chamois. one more gel 15 minutes prior to race time, plus another bottle of water, plus three extra-strength Tylenol, plus visualization, plus let out more air to make it 20 psi in the front and 21 in the rear, plus check the brakes again, plus go to the bathroom one last time, plus two minutes to go, plus breathe and breathe and breathe and fuck I think I need to shit again.

behind the impetus for giving up one lover
is always another: animal or thing to hold
beneath our chest-heave

sometimes the new love isn't flesh is:
a leg over a steel-sleek frame
(gash gap slash badass)

is sugar-skull-and-bone spoke card flap
radical forward motion
is the act
of taking the most efficient machine ever created
and putting it between our thigh-thick

bareback or with a thin
plastic bag over the saddle

is saddle up and zip up into zip-wet
is wet gravel spray up the back
up the legs up
nape to tail

always sometimes
the swap is: yank
is stocking-wad shrivel
and leg-down taxing

other times it's smooth: *sorry this isn't
working it's not you but—*
then the bra's flung   we're bolting
full gallop to leap we get ourselves shelled

this metallic new lover
doesn't do missionary position

she's polyamorous
dirty-full of things
to give she flicks
mud up the shins
quads buttocks
the chin and panting
face the fleshy pounds

of earth-silt clinging the auric
frame clasped by our gapless

while a pale-paunch cloud
(overhead and low)
intermittently spews or sprays
or slush-says something
inappropriate

we'd hawk it all for her:

that brief feeling of
flight: transient rockets / ten
-der herd of glitter—

for the diehard cyclocross fans or the lives of the party or the racers wanting to radiate the antithesis of psi and anxiety shits and giving a fuck, pre-race prep can and does get unserious:

consume large amounts of libations into the small hours of the night before, or the night before the night before, or both. electric daffodil Lonestar or Rainier or PBR broth. shots the morning of or mid-race. flask or joint. dance your face off in a parka in the pouring rain, or in a feather boa, comb-over, and galoshes. heckle until hoarse. cowbell, cowbell, or more cowbell. unicorn and rainbow bootie shorts or stars and stripes thong.

what would the 19th-century French soldier and his fellow copains think. would they check tire pressure with straight-laced expression, slide their feet into flat metal-caged pedals, race like all get-out. or would they grab nips of whiskey and the nipples of half-naked fans, stuff scooped dollars down their woolen jerseys, turn the music up loud, and get down.

the weather

cyclocross is
shit weather is:
thirty-four and raining

is snow is ice
a little wind so the eyelids stick

is sideways sheets
of sleet then sun then
hail then sun then

sleet

is weather
like a wide-open lover (voracious

dripping

relentlessly
kinetic)

so I mouth: make it rain motherfuckers

press the sentiment
against the back of wet

teeth

with my tongue

until the sky
crumples

until the sheets
wring themselves onto

halfzippd slipcleavage
squall over hotpink lovers—
epicene spinsters

is indecisive

weather patterning into all manner of mud
like peanut butter adhering to our lower lips
our eyebrows
the dark tunnels
of our brake-cable housing

to the inside of our chamois
front of our throats
sides of our cheeks
our socks and eyelashes
matted hair

like soup
like grease like
rock crystal

the slip in it wet
(the coffee-ground brown to cindery red
to the kind of yellow that's like dandelion
smear on a forearm)

the wind howling mud into sheer hard-pack
(that sloughs off like skin when skidded)
         into bone-chatter
         because grooves and texture and lather
         solidify in Sunday-sun

         is the season
         of dirt and grime and microbes and smut

soil

         and pebble
         bark decay and crushed leaf
         precious stone and precious
metal

         and polluted rainwater
spit
excrement

oil

         a season of disintegrated bone passing through
         our bodies a lithospheric intimacy
         most can only hope for

         so much so that when the snow season begins
         and there's more and

                   more laundry to do
                   a dark ribbon to be riddn
                   let the sock pile pile

my bones can feel it
they talk about it in chattery syllables of ache
that urge me to check the forecast just so they can say: see
that's what we've been gossiping about

the weather is on its merry way
and my bones and the body that suspends them

pinch

and expand at the same time

everything inside me insists: migrate across the ice field
away from warmer weather
against the grain of geese
because there

is where I'll find the other parts of myself

scattered

among the millions of cold-flurry pixels coming down

next to my bones my heart
moves with the blue-lime and citrine
orange then red-burst coils of forecast

(the earth
and its elements
do wondrous
things)

and our bodies do wondrous things because of them

a single dark cable roping itself
into spirographs in the snow

our bodies atop bicycles
beneath a machined sky and spinning the dark
cable like Arachne in winter

the elements and our bodies at work
the elements and our bodies at play
it all folds to slush by midday then freezes

overnight beneath a handful
of shaved steel

if we take a monochromatic aerial photograph
of the spirograph our bodies make in the snow

and a snapshot of the spirograph our breathing makes
while moving through that snow

and then lay those two images next to a prism
of freshly spun orb-silk
(radial-wet web
of spider ejaculate)

all the sheet music
would look the same
(a respiratory fugue in three movements)

if played percussively the syncopation would remind us
of the feral marrow and fatty gossamer inside our bones

a thumping sound like the faint memory
of the initial bricolage
that was us

frothing / churning out
blood at the helm then cuppd piss
where did it all go—

the race

before we begin we pre-ride:
zip thickly into rain gear
embrace the gritty troposphere
plot lines through circles

after we pre-ride we strip to skin-thick
painted in porous elasticity

and we race

like the sprouted dragon teeth of Cadmus in a sea
of dogged attack

all leg-smeared
in shiny nutmeg embrocation

a spectacle smashing our grace out

spiral to huphup up steps
summoned animals animaling
a bicycle game

where church is the dirt the grass mounds flagged
parceled by police tape and metal barricades
a steeple-less place
where on Saturdays
and Sundays we come to pray

thunder octaves hymns
(spilled beer
life thrusting
itself through the dilated)

psalms pissing out our legs

the hallowed clack of gearshift
sandy dirt in the mouth

come dusk on these days we look up
from our worlds

we sit quietly
enough for long enough
to sense the tilt of a diorama

still
(on its side)

to witness the slow-fold of wet
cardboard walls

and notice the gold
smear-pasting onto a papery
skyline the soaked neighborhood
pushing a grocery cart
into the squint

the geese
honking across a soggy field
our faces thick with earth

we: gather-gathered

on a Sunday we
are not pious everything:
—holy & splitting

competitors not competition
(there's a difference)

and at the end of the day we know:
it's just bike racing

but what's been peddled to us
since birth:
contend

slaughter

legs closed
hush
head down
fold
is a very real joke

so we engage
every cell in our bodies
to pedal through the wet cement
before it dries

flinging towards some whole
beyond & when it's all done—
bawl steel / untame: love

come race day
we are spiderlings

above and all around us
the sky is splitting and the split is puking
and the hard earth turns
into an epidermis of greased unpredictability
hoarfrost-glinting dirt so heroic
it knows not to let go

at first there's the instinct to scurry
scatter
take flight

then a subtle fuck-yes takes over the abdomen
we employ the use of dynamic kiting
extrude several threads into the air

allow ourselves to be carried away by wind

at the close of the domestic cyclocross season
cold January dusk settles in hard

still
we continue to gerbil through shoddy
iced-over or snowed-on or frozen rut-mud
discarded shoelace loops

near the end of a season
the things we weren't sure we had learned
begin to surface
the bright minutes the bullet holes
all the things we fucked up

theatre-style
butter-sun barely chucks itself
across the last races of the last days

for those of us still riding in numb circles
cinder
blocks for limbs and several inches
of thermal insulation and wool
swaddling our muscle our
bone
we take stock
unbuckle and sob and sense maybe
what it means maybe
to follow through

because as serious
and as unserious as we make it

we are still fistfuls
of childhooded adults
pedaling through dusk-fields
as fast as we can
laughing

and at some point or another it's inevitable
we all step through just step

into the Amer
-ican experiment—oh /
look: all burn all wheel

the he-men / strip

Velo-swift bell lap

sweat

to the men clad in spandex
you know who you are

dollar bill to my teeth and a flush

tongue to your calves / quads
pedaled into pear bulge steepd
in sunrust & damp

with your cloudboom laughter

slingshot through beardthick
& head back eyes flinging: rock
-ets, copper & dusk

          hotfoot to bolt
chest-heave and your

                                        haunch like what beneath
                                        spandex lucence, hips that flick
                                        me on—demount *this*

what is it to be stripped

to strip
something

to the skin and make a break for it
sprint a beeline to the ocean
at ten past midnight in the sweat of August

the soft pads of our soft feet eating
up the pavement the pebble (the splinter)
then the sand the crushed shell the soft seaglass
the lukewarm salt-wet
swell of bioluminescence and earthmilk
rising up to meet
our naked brawn

the clump of still-warm clothes
crumpled beneath a street lamp
about a quarter-mile back

stripping down like slitting
what we were supposed to be or how
we thought we'd never

the exodus leaving salt rings
on our shirts the sides of our cheeks
our temples like all the he-mans

o wagons of speed
men enough to prance to shave—
let your tangle down

while the lavender between

your thighs remains still
the scarwrists tatwrappd: planets
anchors / women / stars

to be stripped for sex
and stripping for fuck and
fuck what we were told

to be stripped down
in the name of celerity

as if it's somehow always faster
when we've been plucked to nothing
and our skin is

sore

our grey matter lucid-raw

to be pestled and peeled and dismantled
down to our bright rinds

to be gutted

and when is it that we
get to be utterly in love with ourselves

the throttle slips
over and over

and then to be stripped some more

the bell lap

this is a burning cave and then the world
in flames beyond the cave

breath plumes out
chests and rib cages
well and cleave

where and when to rip the seam of the old edge
find something new find the white line
and cross it first

seconds into minutes into a thick booklet of years
a tide recedes and a flashbulb goes off
at the same time everything crescendo everything

beyond the body falls away
the way rain falls on a shock of wet
torsos beating forward through salt-chop

a fountain or an open hydrant
in the middle of a field

every pedal stroke pulling
at the fur of adolescence

the bell lap is either years away
or it comes too soon and nothing
is not on fire

something shatters
drives and curls
into the white heat of trying
harder and smarter
than the time before last

the thing about my father

addiction (that usurper)
it fills the form of: adrenaline-opiate
gamble-sex and straight no chase

work
sunless tanning

those days
when two wheels feels like breathing
like an extension of my working
body like when I was a kid
(swearing I could ride all night and
into the moon)

running out
of gears to shift into and still
wanting more

no such thing as enough
my legs half-peregrine half-fox
half-hummingbird with sailfish quads
hunting prey

feeling absolutely nothing
except that I can do anything
my lines are clear I'm so
goddamn high

sugared sequin-eyes
wanting to love it all
into my life

sometimes
after the rush
of a day or a year of wringing legs and
hearts and hearts

after the neon minutes of
what am I racing towards or away from and what
does a few seconds faster even mean

fuck

how much higher
do I need to get

at the close of a season
after the competitive focus
that's like microprocessing
with the hundred eyes of Panoptes

there's a sort of coming down

I know
it's nothing
like what my father went through
those years

he drank his body
into a nervous breakdown and broke
into himself
and had to be cinched down
at the wrists

long enough
for the bright scorch
to dilute

for the cursing
the balled fists the balled body
the bawling
to reach a glazed lull

so much to hold:

raw husks beating on—
how goldheavy to live through
this life / not around

after another season
of doing something I'm not even sure
I still want to be doing
but that is reprieve and magnify
at the same time is something
my muscles remember my body
returns to without fail

coming down
is nothing like my father's broken nerves

still
when the season ends I'm:

in the shower wearing a soiled spandex costume
watching the dirt of blurred days suck down the drain

my quartz-sobs
pliant in the steam the soap
the scrubbing

the hot shower pelting
my fetal the image
of my father splayed

shaking

my mother and a child on her hip
coaxing
her clothes getting soaked

the training / away

teal glitter in my eyes
slices of chuckle
caught at the back of my throat

aeronautics
cropping up in my bones

the roads to rove the paved roads
that make me feel faster
younger than I really am

until everything I couldn't seem to change
becomes a tiny dot in the way-back distance

and then all those tiny dots become one small pinprick
in a sea of violent clouds at my back

so I keep turning
the pedals over and over
and over until that pinprick
becomes a pixel disintegrating
into the violent

later
when the whole world begins to piss its warm rain
I swallow the pixel pinprick made up of far-off dots
slide it down my throat whole

I listen to the roads preach:
fuck it
to the hills in a mottled caravan

coin purse empty / tossd—
forget: all there is to know
live the vagaries

the movement over chipsealed roads
that turn into gravel roads
that rattle and lose

red clay and silt roads like streamers
let loose through parched egg-yolk fields
(have you ever ridden through dried gold)
the shimmer-dust sticking to my body like matte bronzer
darkening in my sweat

granite and limestone
dirt and root
all manner of surface
I just want to lick
to taste to feel
the texture and history of by way of tongue

sometimes taste is the only way to get through to myself
so I kneel down and gloss the surface with my open mouth
let my body plot things out
using the crumple of maps and blueprints
tucked into the trifold pocket of my heart

still
I'm lost inside the violet light
I had forgotten things pleat
in gradients that never end

we end: in every
legshow city—continue
the way to undone

thank you, death

I've witnessed the ground-flight
of the silver fox
as it led me down so many desolate trails
bounding inches from my own respiring body

I've seen the red fox
in canyons far below
and right beside me sprinting
reminding me of something

I've ducked to avoid the low swoop
of a hoot owl diving for forest mice
(those muted grey windup cars
testing their luck through crushed pine needle and loam)
then watched as he ascended back to watching

I've ridden through the deep woods long enough
and with my eyes wide enough
to come close enough to snakes and spiders
and mushrooms whose kaleidoscope colors
and patterns proclaim:
I could have your life like *that*

I've smelled the immense heft of it
before it came into view:
a mother and her black cubs
smudging a dim-wet forest
(furred charcoal thumbprints
on the verge of streak)

I've felt the ground-thunder
of a herd of elk taking off like minnows up a knoll
(a school of antler and hoof buffeting
into the matte distance)

I've startled an entire hillside of cattle
watched it shift like ginger-colored sea anemone
flagging in current

my legs alternating between pedal
and coast
my eyes fixed to theirs

it feels foreign or inconceivable
how there will come a time

when everything just stops

I think about this a lot
the stopping

and about how everything might continue
elsewhere into the undulating distance

that's never not there:
dramatic gravity / am
-ethyst remembrance—

a fist steadying a Krylon can
over the side of a boxcar

a child wading
        into a river

        me dropping
        to my hands and knees

        in the snow
        and saying thank you

thank you
thank you

        because sometimes I just want to feel:

        something heal in this
        squall the beyondbeyond &
        shimmy from the furl—

I've been there
(pedaling into the warmth just before dawn)
                when the ragtag coyote shakes from the sagebrush
                muscles herself across an unlined road

                and then at dusk
                when one coyote croons
                and becomes eleven

                like flecks of metal sucking towards a magnet
                they appear from seemingly nowhere
                a chorus of yip-howls at my back

                I've circled back
                and stopped on the sides of roads
                to inspect freshly deceased birds
(their chests still warm)
                their reptilian legs not yet stiffened

                I've inspected the iridescence of their wingspan
                the specific patterning in each feather
                the creamy down and semi-plume underneath
                their small soft heads

                I've felt the welling in my chest
                and in my throat at how supple
                how swift this world can be

if I close my eyes for a second
I see flashes of a start line
I see all the other cyclists lined up
ready for the gun to go off

then
when I open my eyes
I'm pedaling back towards sunset
powerful beasts beating at the earth next to me

the two images overlay one another
all I see are thick lashes
warm breath showing itself in frozen air

gentility

fear
the way they gallop alongside

me / glovd hand to rough
thickneck: almost I could al
-most jump on ride in

a fear that's

in the throats in the
backs of the knees in the fight—
flutter-flight then lull—

the what it comes down to

you and I dears   we are part of the animal club   only it's not a club
it's everywhere in the margins
        in between the grass blades   we are a kingdom
of creatures practicing a fierce kind of love
a love that involves long hours pedaling bicycles   ripping
one another's legs off while counting seconds as if they were years
yes   my thick mistresses   my

                    buffalo leggd She
                    -ras / grotesque flexd doebullets—
                    gloss holeshot showdowns

we slip into it:
scorpion-pink baselayers and David Bowie

we are x dressd in
renegade piratelight—
Athena's sphinxes

lioness bodies
fiery heads full of teeth
and warrior-gold eyeshadow
fanged light and pierce shooting
from our bandwidth

fully armed we bust
straight out of Zeus's thick skull
(scuffed figurines finding our way)

we are brass and bold and more than

grass stuck to the chin
cognizant bloodshot & we—
tunnel ignition

ours is a love   that means sewing one another's legs back on
   with care   and in the rain and then talking
to each other and to the Universe
even if it's through tears   our love involves tears

and when the human ache staring back at you becomes an open circuit
of sheet lightning   and flashbulb
do not avert your body   discard your heartstrings
   close your eyes on the pulsing
creature before you
instead gather it all in
the heat
sit with it
engage

(what else is there)

ACKNOWLEDGMENTS

Pages 81–83 ("I've been there . . . flutter-flight then lull—") were published in *boneshaker*, issue #20.

the outro / shout-out track

extreme and deep everything to:
the fierce golden light that is Arielle Greenberg / you said yes and I believed you and that's all I needed

love to those without whom *bell lap* would not have been possible:
TC Tolbert (H E A R T!!!) / Emily Carr / T. Geronimo Johnson / my special po' heads / Michael Broder / Indolent Books – thanks for taking me in

ride or die love to:
my Jersey Shore Fam (especially AJ)
my brother – for being fucking awesome and for giving me that old Klein hardtail way back when / you created a monster
dad – for putting a wrench in my hand always and telling me *you do it* / pops you are more than just a part of this / I am proud of you for coming through
mom/yoma/my best friend since before birth – for your momentum your unending laughter your ability to see others / you are an Artist to the core / a gorgeous force
Jamesy – for always thinking and challenging and loving hard / for championing poetry and fuck the man and adventure / for your feminism and your smile
my Southern Fam – for a generosity I cannot describe / for the means and the love and your tender-tender hearts

more than gratitude to:

Marcel – for your words in your voice in my head at every race

Marisa Crawford / Lee Ann Roripaugh / Lisa Jarnot – for taking a chance and reading

brother Sacha & The Vanilla Workshop – for building golden unicorn bicycles with bare hands/hearts/minds and for bankrolling this dirty cyclocross racer like a boss

Jeff Motherfucking Curtes – all the love

the wolfpack / wolves everywhere / especially Earthquaker – for tough love

Art and Ellen / my Jersey Squad – for opportunity generosity and so much muddy joy

R. Luciano – for resilience support and hard work

Martin – your words to my 11-yr-old me changed the course of everything

a bowed head to:

my Muses my sister-goddesses – for teaching me for making me dance sing feel move think / feel alive when it gets dark / being here with me

Jay Z / K. Lamar / Chance / jazz / DMST / punk / hip hop / Basquiat / ALL the poets and writers and visual artists and musicians who have come before me

to:

really good coffee everywhere

cyclocross you crazy motherfucker

snow

the Jersey streets and forests that raised me / never let me not pay attention

New Brunswick alleycat races / Rosener and Bedoya and Oakes

Vernor and his film "Pure Sweet Hell" / saw that shit and fell in love

'til the wheels fall off

ABOUT THE AUTHOR

 Laura Winberry is a feminist poet, essayist, and visual artist residing in Bend, Oregon. Born and raised in New Jersey, she still pronounces "coffee" and "water" as one might expect. With two other poets, she co-operates The Stay Project, an online space for experiences as they relate to the current POTUS. Laura also races cyclocross domestically and internationally for Speedvagen, a hand-built bicycle company based in Portland, OR. She attended Rutgers University and received her MFA from OSU-Cascades. *bell lap* is her first book of poetry.

ABOUT INDOLENT BOOKS

Indolent Books is a small poetry press founded in 2015 and operating in Brooklyn, N.Y. We publish work that is innovative, provocative, and risky. We cultivate underrepresented voices and are committed to the values of diversity and inclusion. While open to all, we maintain a special focus on queer poets and poets over 50 without a first book. Indolent Books is an imprint of Indolent Arts Foundation, Inc., a 501(c)(3) nonprofit charity founded in 2017.

CPSIA information can be obtained
at www.ICGtesting.com
Printed in the USA
LVHW091818130220
646864LV00006B/1168